Adoptee Song

Maria S. Picone

Adoptee Song

ISBN: 979-8-9899400-4-2

www.gameoverbooks.com

"Current-borne, wave-flung, tugged hugely
by the whole might of ocean…"

-Ursula K. LeGuin

"Angel of God, my guardian dear,
to whom His love commits me here,
ever this day, be at my side
to light and guard, to rule and guide."

-"Angel of God," Catholic Prayer to the Guardian Angel

Table of Contents

III: Wings

Foreward

"I have no idea how it coheres." This searingly honest line in the tellingly titled "History of Adoption in ~~Korea~~ Maria" primes us for the intellect, music, and central query of *Adoptee Song*. Is it possible for multiple senses of identity to cohere? Is there logic to be found in incoherence? In poems that range from playfully experimental to experimentally intentional, Maria S. Picone writes of "two different names," declaring "I am the eternal river, perpetuity of mirrors flowing forever" ("朝鮮姓名復舊令"). This tendency towards multiplicity, perpetuity, is reflected in Maria's authorial strengths: dense syntax that refuses white legibility, fearless engagements with a wide array of free verse forms, and an appreciation of word play that I firmly believe can only come from those of us to whom English and/or America remain, permanently, at arm's length.

But keeping the reader at arm's length does not interest Maria as a poetic approach. Reader, I have found myself saying the word "generous" a lot these unwinding "post"-pandemic days—thanking those around me for their time, attention, care. So I thought quite intentionally about using it here. I asked myself, "Am I simply defaulting back to calling Maria's writing *generous* because it is the easiest thing to say?" On a third, fourth, fifth read of this chapbook, I determined such a critique could not be leveraged. For Maria *is* a generous writer—and these poems are outpourings of that generosity. Not just in her willingness to—even insistence on—painting for the reader an incredibly detailed picture of the intersections of her identity; no, Maria's generosity is syntactical, formal, imagistic, sonic, feminist. What she says she is in these poems, she gives us in this chapbook: "another shell on the reef: another shell" (Hypnerotomachia).

To read *Adoptee Song* is to be rocked by a lullaby of lost worlds, to be held in the place between slumber and attention; as she writes in the poem "History of Adoption in ~~Korea~~ Maria," "I became a doorway without country, swinging open and shut." Indeed, Maria's language swings open and shut throughout the text, crossing through phrases to comment on a culturally mixed identity as in "the rough draft of my life," including the Korean alphabet and explicit commentary on her limited understanding of it throughout the text. I am grateful for these poems—how direct and incisive their knowledge of both the self and the self's limitations, how playful they can be, and ultimately, how honest they are about their version of the Asian American experience. As Maria writes of our complexities and contradictions in "For my own 34th Birthday," "I can say it in twelve languages but I can never answer."

Raena Shirali

I: Child's Play

To Fievel from *An American Tail*

You are a child like me, young & trusting,
gazing up at moon & stars in longing
for family, dream praying to the guardian
angel. We space-worn immigrants carry American tales,
journeys of ecstasy//terror reeling in fledging nightmares.

I fear shadowy warriors with spears assaulting my bed,
my father's skull cracking in half, me with only a Band-Aid
to press back against the rift. A cast of stuffed animals
& imaginary friends witness my sleepless quietude,
my doubt that family awaits me—or has forgotten me.

Unlike you, I've never found my mother
's hug again. I've been in this bedroom waiting, forever aware she passed
me on from her womb, alternate future

portending   dislocating

me from her body like a fallen star. Knowing my tale
began with the crossing from Seoul to Boston. She passed
on me. My only wish, as I behold the angel's silver visage:
for her to be *thinking of me, loving me tonight.*

Time moves on, but in this sacred limbo part
of me will always linger—this quiet belief if I'm perfect
enough, if I endure I might make it home.
Underneath the stars dawn birds are ramping up
their singing; *somewhere out there*

I will find the person whose love committed me here
I will be by the side of the angel, the guardian
for whom now, tears welling up in an old child's eyes

I have to believe is asleep *underneath the same big sky.*

1986 년 October

10 월 thirtieth

30 일 1986

my   ears   into

       foreign language

    entered

swaddled in this pink baby

tongue   I

      western civilization

inhaled   this popping, staccato

tempo   samulnori drums   red   rounded

apples—A for apples,

A for astrological abecedarian—I

broke through   first language   barrier

constellated I, paradox,

membrane

placenta to placenta

no longer one   plethora of twos suspended in space

time, entered October 30th from the 31st, calculated

difference accounting for day

light savings time, became   cancer

sun scorpio   moon   in transit fighting   한국 phonemes

[retrograde]

just when I entered this house no one can say,

how many revolutions

-worth of fallout I had to dodge

questioning. when you bow to the earth you are pointing,

X-axis bend from the waist you swoop around cosmos

inclining to

gratitude, acknowledgement, respect

you mark yourself on a trajectory of

unbelonging. I learned

Korea   from this distance

othering myself

towards   a new identity   unable to

verify my birth time, birth

zodiac.

not to bow   I learned

to stay still   stay

awake   at midnight   pronounce

American   myself

        to stop   [mourning]

the tiger of my youth

wondering where   had gone

welcoming twelve other animals   I

traded these

        rats & roosters

for   crabs & scorpions,

dragon   for

virgin   relinquished

my horse   for

a pitcher of water.

To the ugly duckling, newly hatched

As you crack your seed
-ling body into world
mother warmth abandons
you, subjunctive fog
covered waters to fear//swim;
keep han wings, nalgae
tucked by your sides.

Kick your boat feet
until you can't see
the size of your difference. Look
beyond pond
-mirrored face you question.

Do not fear, swim.   Han//ala
Do not fear, swim.   날//ala

How You Were Lucky

You weren't an abortion.

You didn't have to shave, despite your mom's warnings.

You found out early a body can be a commodity.

You didn't suffer the trauma of growing up Korean
poor?

You didn't eat kimchi or other "ethnic foods"
until high school, when your loved ones
told you it stank.

You were adopted by a white family,
in the land of the free, with complete paperwork
& therefore not deported.

You didn't have to learn how to be a minority in the US
until later, when you had to self-study
how your face wasn't just a face.

You feel this.

You feel this way.

You feel this, weighing the lucks against the lacks.

at play I handbraided origin stories

from popsicle sticks & glitter pipecleaners
too marooned from the coast of my birth,
the shore of my family, the shoal of a certain reef
& what the universe gave me back was: The Trailer
!

Seabrook, NH, salt waves colliding, rocking in me
the sand pail of my heart. Hampton Beach sludge sand
in my gut. to me the stars were not a river
but grains of time lost as I cavorted on the painted horse
at the campground playground. "Maria, big sound!"
my mom's best friend would shout, smashing coconut
into pineapple in her Hadron machine. when my mom tucked
me in, I'd recoil, "Mom, you have booze breath!"

though all the kinetics of the ocean would not
bear back that which I ceaselessly lost,
if I could ride fireworks & fried dough highs
I could return home for a while. if the pop
rocks of a station wagon crunching C Road
can't take me there, what can? once,
I cried all the way home, that 1.1 hours
atypical for me, a kid who had borne all
in silence, & my mom discovered I had stolen
those road stones in my diaper, hiding away
the heavy weight of a child's sorrow. oh, how it looks
the same on Google Earth!

Antipodes

From you I
descended
to the other side of the globe
bones of

skin in snow
in three sets of han clothes
I remember
underneath this tabula rasa

all I did
even if you deny

through cracks in your system
I fell
I crawled up
North America

you covered me
you erased me
torrent, spray, swimming
this orphan
-age child remembers
even if you forget
what I had to do to live

What Is, Enough

Once I knew not to expect a Hollywood ending,
I realized the hero's journey never finishes.
In a drama, I might find my birth parents and reunite
in an epilogue that fulfills my unvoiced longing.

Here on my planet, a Korean girl could dream to aim
so high as to find a loving family to kneel with at dinner;
for each adoptee given back to an origin leapfrogged
as a baby, a hundred close the file with a sigh.

Mine too, manila folder creased by questioning hands:
my dad's handwriting MARIA—KOREA, the fingertips
of a girl young enough to believe stories of lost princesses,
a fledgling flapping wings in her mythical return.

These candied symphonies spun of moonlight sugar
spiral us into anticipation for the heart-thing: resolution—
instead, in life, the answers flit like ghosts at dark
crossroads, like an unresolved chord hanging…

For that reason, like a villain, I rail against my ending—
fighting the fury with the furor of fighting against a dare
to believe. *Sometimes*, at a doubtful 3 am, the universe has
no drama but your mom texting, "Go to bed!"

History of Adoption in ~~Korea~~Maria

"In South Korea, adoption was initially introduced to find families to look after war orphans and mixed-race children, and has gone through a series of changes over the past 50 years. The nation's economic development and improved quality of life have led to a rise in domestic adoption, enhancing the public perception of adoption. Recently, the South Korean government designated the National Adoption Day."

-Korea Adoption Services Website

당신은 한국인이 아닙니다

At four months old, I relinquished my rights as a Korean citizen. I became a doorway without country, swinging open and shut.

당신은 한국인이 아닙니다

2012 Special Adoption Law: "The Government shall endeavor to reduce the number of Korean children adopted abroad," the law states, "as part of its duties and responsibilities to protect children."

엄마, 아빠 날 지켜줘!

January 1954. My mom's birthday.

Mommy protect me. Daddy protect me.

You, stand on shifting, ground. You stand on shifting, ground. You, stand on, shifting ground.

June 25. My birthday.

Mommy Korea, Daddy America.

The land fractures. The land fractures. The land fractures. The land in you.

1961. My father graduates from high school.

Mommy America; Daddy Korea.

당신은 변화하는 땅에 서 있습니다.

1976. My parents meet.

땅이 부서졌습니다.

1997. I enter junior high school.

Pencil in your rights. Pencil in your rights, Pencil in your rights. Pencil in your name.

I have two names. I do not have two names.

여 is a sound like a grimace. Open your mouth wide at both corners. 여 is the "over" ten adoptees in 1954.

우리는 한국인이 아닙니다.

Ink in your rights. Sharpie in your rights. Superglue your rights. Chisel your name.

여 is for the sound in 영: practice it over and over. Over ten times. Over thousands of times.

Your heart turns over before you say it. 영영영영. The unlucky number is four.

7,275 children were adopted overseas in the 1960s. 48,247 in the 1970s. 65,321 in the 1980s.

두 가지 이름이 있습니다.

여 is the over 65,000 adoptees. The annual average was 6,532.

Every year they emptied out a town. Every year they fractured a university. Every year.

The Korean government has designated the third wave of adoptions as 'A Leap into Professional Adoption Projects and Child Services.'

I am a professional adoption project. You can Scrum me, don't worry. The government's phrasing will not harm me:

국적회복허가 신청서.

I am not a diaspora. I am. You stereotype me but Korean food is one of the only tenets I can authentically embody.

I am an amateur Korean speaker. I rely on big corporations to speak my sentences. 여 is my sticking sound. When there are Koreans I shut my mouth. I do not open its corners wide.

I have no idea how it coheres. 저는 한국 여성입니다.

the rough draft of my life

my mother always made me finish my ~~kimchi~~ broccoli,
drink ~~red ginseng tonic~~ orange juice for my health.

my ~~halmoni~~ mémère made ~~army~~ beef stew;
my father's mother asked me, "Have you eaten yet?"

sometimes we went into ~~Busan~~ Boston, the big city,
to gaze out at the harbor's colorful ships;

if we wished to use another language, we exclaimed
a ~~Merry Christmas~~ Buon Natale, &, when asked

now what it was like, I answer, ~~"like everyone."~~
"not like everyone." ~~Italian~~ Korean heritage set me apart

from friends even whose ancestors spoke only English.
how lucky to feast on dueling revisions, magpies & storks,

to grow up, to grow into—

II: Names

Adoption by CEFR Level

<u>A1: Breakthrough or beginner</u>

I am Maria.
I am from America. I am from Korea.

My family is from America. My family is from Korea.
I am from Korea, but my family is from America.

I am American.
Well, I am Korean. But I am American.

My family comes from Italy. I come from Korea.
They do not live in Italy. They do not live in Korea.

No, my family lives in America.
No, my father is not Korean.

No, I do not have Korean relatives.
No, I do not know my Korean relatives.

A2: Waystage or elementary

I live in Myrtle Beach. My hometown is Leominster.
My birth city is Jinhae-si. Now it is called Jinhae-gu.

I went to Korea. It is lovely. I came
to the USA to live with my family.

Every day I think about Korea. I think about
visiting. I think about living, and loving, and leaving.

I think about a poem I read. I feel
sad. Every day I meet new people.

They ask
questions.

B1: Threshold or intermediate

I made my pain into a passable conversation. I read classic literature with a glossary. I painted my feelings in flag colors: black, red, white, blue. I started to combine, mix paints, iterate on sentence structure. I impressed you with some vocabulary while falling down on grammar. I considered the words I cannot spell in any language, the unique sounds that expelled themselves from my ancestral mouths. That nameless sensation, that thing you lack the words for, that exists. What you think of as language is just a wound.

B2: Vantage or upper intermediate

I have not yet achieved this level on the back of my heritage, not yet let my ancestors carry me up over this hill. I see the cliff ahead of me, the promised view, the just rewards. I see an AirBnB in my great-grandfather's hometown, cherry blossoms and salt water. In hypotheticals, if I had been born in any other place, I would not yet have traced the lines of my bones tremoring under the earth. Had I known either more or less than what I now exactly know, I could have never adopted so many other ugly duckling languages to float in the pond in my hometown's neighborhood. I could have gone fishing under the ice. But those swans circling around my identity—백조 cygne cigno 白鳥, theyah's no friggin' swans heyah.

C1: Effective operational proficiency or advanced

we are all crying
out for something. we are all
cries in crisis—call us, *humans*—we none
of us have never cried, no one
crystallizes with their crystal
eyes a lack of cry. I, too, cry

over the past; I cry inside a happy moment
to watch it die; I cry with the anguish of family,
the hurricane of my history, the jet lag rising
fast within me, echo of the places in me,
passport to the trauma in me, generations spilling
tears within me. bitter-tongued, I taste these
crystal droplets, and I cry.

C2: Mastery or proficiency

[...]

When to Use 영

영 is a forever I express in null set silence.

I carry my 영 to the second place like a good math Asian.

Though Fahrenheit is right,
I pinpoint melting point of water 영.

영 is English language given voice by Korean spirit.

I slip 영 through the hourglass
of barley teakettle, barley teacup.

I sweat with 영 pronunciation in front of real Koreans.

I grimace in steep frown of 영 that escaped
me in this melting pot.

I refer to how I lost time with myself—that precious grain.

영 sum game of adding and subtracting
what's gained and lost.

영 stands for the o and double o's
of anglicized Picone, Soo.

영 is the termination of a name begun in land, in water 水.

영 is the termination of a name I no longer hold, name
born in water, 수.

영 is the termination of a name that belonged
to a Korean, 수영.

Sometimes I Feel I Am a Shell Living Inside Another Woman's Skin

she, like a big Labrador,
suburban *have-to-have,* did well,
papers in a manila folder
after they background-checked her
new mom and dad. forever home
she couldn't choose
stamped on her dog tags, intimate
stranger to universal-American white
life. fixed her.

Maria Picone, oppressively Italian—
insists that they say, "Pih co ni,"
not "Pi co nay." buzzy wasps
replace this "ne" with a NEIGH
like a horse saying, NAY—
father had a store: Pic One.

discomfort loud among *them,*
bronzed women awash with white insights,
Barbies wined out in the writing workshop
waiting for her to represent
her tribe of purported Labradors
and -doodles

but friends,
Maria S. Picone doesn't fit
in the utensil drawer with those silverware
gals who spent the pandemic baking;
the Pottery Barn carries no chopsticks.
Maria S. Picone doesn't need your surprised eyebrows
punctuating the more perfect union
of her name and her person—

can't be helped by obedience school,
is disinterested in your *inspiring virtual conversation*
on enjambment, erasure, hands-on experience
of Asian silence. Maria S. Picone
doesn't need the squints of a roomful of POC
wondering if this Jindo got squeezed
into the wrong kennel,
an explanatory husband hovering in the Zoom
with a "Beh!" or "Madonna!" for this epic
mis-racing

[*moment of respect*]

misconception that she stole an imaginary
woman's name to gloss a blanched veneer
onto her gold skinned body,
that she is a shell from exotic shores,
bleached of inconvenient remnants
of color. forever stealing another's bones.
always in the doghouse. friends,
please realize: the origin story of Maria S.
Picone is not yours to choose,
assume, scribble out,

white
out

Language Immersion

I take this harsh   foreign   thing
birth   right birth   mark birth
language   into my body   in usual ways:
K-drama   K-pop   K-phantoms half
remembered

                        hauntings of han childhood
tongue twisting   completing my sentence
spitting   blood between bewildered teeth

                        failed transplants
my body   my blood   rejects
my bloody   dismembered
        Korean[-eo]

once I was: pure   holy   spotless   han-speaking
brought to limbo//foster home
forgetting phonics of baby babble   외국
waiting months to embrace   미국
English from zero

passing   in the first year of life
I, a fetus,   sinned

32

yet there is no one to say

         this is my body

which will be given up

         to life after death   ***in America***

no one to carry these sins but me,

sorry to be born

sorry to have caused this shame

sorry with guilt of carrying & having carried this language

my Korean   my words

do not do you   justice

it is truly right to give

you thanks & praise   mother

Korea

why give reparation when there's nothing

to repair

Loki & me

"It seems that all that was good has died/and is decaying in me..."
-Disturbed, "Down with the Sickness"

the feels when you can look at the TV and say, that was low-
key me. not gonna lie, I'm not so whitewashed that I'm the
only raven-haired sorcerer in a warrior-king family, not so
colonized that my blood runs blue with frost runes and light
ning blonds. I'm one generation away from an Italian boy at a
white high school, microaggressions passed on to me: Italian
stallion, Italian Korean. I'm from a different war

-torn country, bisected like the Bifrost under great ringing
blows of geopolitics. but you opened up your hate and let it
flow into me, onscreen, nauseated by the knowledge we didn't
fit into a family. even one that wanted us. that struck me hard
as Mjolnir—was I not here

to be entertained?—as these little jokes meant for fun ("he's
adopted!") tore a portal to the dark wilds of a heart. othered
monsters for white heroes to beat

down. & the world laughed at our ridiculousness, Hulk-
smashed into an outline of our broadest corners. we writhed
in pain on concrete comfort asking, "what more than
that?"—we painted the silver screen black dealing with these
changes, living with [   ] & we became: more

of ourselves, more of contradiction. the world is a scary
place; the nine realms of silence rule strong. race [   ].
colony [   ]. government [   ]. woken up, the
demon in us, the truth. NGO [   ]. contractual [   ].
birth family [   ]. erased & reclaimed, you willingly
fell. mom, Queen [   ]. dad, King [   ].
adopted, pawn [   ]. we can never achieve nostos; we
will always be homing back to that which never wanted us. &
when I dream

보다

or

I am going to tell you how much I like watching movies and reading books until I learn Korean

with this found poem in Japanese taken from the Jisho dictionary entry for the type of simple verbs I know in Korean,

because I am too chickenshit to actually attend lessons and this is a cry for help because I just wasted more of my life relearning basic Korean for the nth time

1. to see; to look; to watch; to view; to observe

えいがをみたり、ほんをよんだり

I SEE (that) I am Korean. I FIND (that) I am not Korean.

2. to examine; to look over; to assess; to check; to judge

かんこくごをまなびなおして

I TRY to learn how to do it all properly, HAVE A GO AT sprinkling Korean identity like gochugaru throughout my life. I GIVE this reclaimed being A TRY.

3. to look after; to attend to; to take care of; to keep an eye on

こころのけんこう

I EXPERIENCE sweat-soaked nightmares of translating word for otherword to some stern songsaengnim's disapproval. I MEET WITH standards that size me up or down until I am never enough.

4. to experience; to meet with (misfortune, success, etc.)

かんこくにいたことがあるん

I LOOK AFTER the erased self blotted into my shadow. I ATTEND TO this Korean body's wants, needs, last. I TAKE CARE OF this Easter basket of microaggressions I pulled on scavenger hunt; I KEEP AN EYE ON their innocuous pastels, waiting for dragons to hatch.

5. to try ...; to have a go at ...; to give ... a try

かんこくごをまなんでみた

I EXAMINE the quaver of my vocal cords, interrogating the integrity of the basic equipment. I LOOK OVER old materials in an attempt to remember birth han. I ASSESS the nervous chill at the nape of my neck; I CHECK my audio quality. I JUDGE myself, and, as in cliché, find wanting.

6. to see (that) ...; to find (that) ...

じゅうぶんになることはできない

I SEE the delicate letters for the first time, the geometry of failure in right angles. I LOOK into the abyss of my misunderstanding; I WATCH my soul augment, infarct, grovel. I VIEW many beginner videos like impressionist clouds passing me by. I OBSERVE my lips and jaw forming a note of pure multivocal truth in this muddled world.

A Note on Reduction and Self-Acceptance

I am not suicidal because I am Korean.
I am not suicidal because I am an adoptee.
I am not suicidal because I am a model minority.
I am not suicidal because I am abnormal.
I am not abnormal.

I am not suicidal because one day in the first grade,
a kid told me, "You look so weird!"
I am not suicidal because one day in the fourth grade,
a boy called me a "chink."
I am not suicidal because one day in high school,
a teen girl said I was an alien.
I am not suicidal because one day in college,
a young man confided in me he hated brown skin.

I am not suicidal because a plethora of -isms wriggled
under my skin.
I am not suicidal because the men who sought to fuck me

began with "Ni hao."
I am not suicidal because of the miracles I pulled out of my pocket to buy
passage to now.

I am not suicidal because of what you did.
Even if you think so.
I am not suicidal because I am flawed.
I am not flawed.

Hypnerotomachia Mariae

I had been considering   today

becoming   a refugee

into bright   deep   sky   wild

-erness no longer   crowned with stars

it is the thousands   dead   I was considering

if you would take

me   the terra nullius Waves oscillate/reverse   Not long

before that little   peninsula   across

seeks to recede   blood into its heart   notices   me

says   Oh   I have been meaning   to write

a postcard How fare   you this fine evening   as I retch

out Americana   overseas Korean   Two poles

stake my tent   over   sea   continent   sea

Territory   I can claim/does not claim me If I die

rock me west   ward   or do as the old

whalers   Unfurl   me down   old Mass beachhead

I have been considering   how to shed

my skin   I have been on   logistics   all day

donations/rubbish for   the curb Induce current

flow in this changing   field/self I

                read once whalers

stranded   ate all the turtles   the wild birds

the birds eggs

        bugs & lichen & moss

    bones   sand   the hand of a dead

crewmate   sloughing off   blackened skin

to feast on raw red

substance When the island became   shivering   naked

    they gazed at the mirror they   made

from   shell scraps   tidal guilt

hit like wave   still they prayed

hard & grave Then into that   stripped

down   bareness   plunged

             a soul

I am considering becoming   this   sea

-faring   refuge   where I will lay down as bones & purity

another shell on the reef

    another shell

朝鮮姓名復舊令

(조선 성명 복구령/Name Restoration Order)

i.
in which the poet prays to her namesake

Ave, Maria, girl full of grace. Thou, beloved, wished-for child, who
crossed the transnational sea.

Blessed art thou among children,
chosen from among our half-country's poorest lands.

Blessed is the fruit of thy virtual pen, Microsoft Word, showering with
formatting woes these selfsame fruits.

Banished, outcast, and reviled, you cover up the girl Ellen,
the plea of the suppliant child. Maria, girl of oft-changing

name, reflecting our Western cultural institutions. Ill-fated
name, bitter name. Pray for us, at the hour of our death,

that we realize your rebellious nature
comes from our sins.

ii.
in which the poet obeys a request to 創氏改名 (창씨개명),
create a surname and change your given name

two different names
I lived under
in the same country
Kim, commonplace, most Korean 김
ubiquitous as 김치
peppering the tables of every
family register, every family restaurant

피코니 broke into this
wielding two uncommon consonants,
P for pillar holding up Greco-Roman
letters, K like the tines of 포크,
interpolating implement. long name
resonant like a tuning fork(u),
down up down. 마리아 too
bookends with vowels, ah and i.
in the middle, there is always 수
consistency of being, Kim 수 Young,
Maria 수 Picone.

iii.
*in which the poet lists some epithets and nicknames belonging
to herself (incomplete)*

AJ
Adrienne/Adriana
shadowdancer9027
Ajantis Scipio
SooP
Maria from Korea
mpicone@_____.edu
Airam
mp15@_____.edu
Maria-teacher
Soo Young
mspicone
"Maria Soo Picone, full of macaroni"

iv.
*in which the poet assembles her name from a list
of possible meanings in* 한자

I am the eternal hero. A perpetuity of glory. My river flows like a mirror,
a projection of forever. I am an outstanding harvest. I gather water to
myself for the flood. I shine in splendor, glorious reflection of a hero
who gave himself to the flood, the river, the water. I am swimming in
liquid. I am a movie that plays me at my bravest, that makes me the hero
of the water. I am perpetually in flower. I swim in this river that waters
the flowers. I reflect the river shining in the luxury of the palace with the
cherry blossoms; I drift down that waterway to my destiny. I flood; I still
have harvest outstanding. I am an echo, a projection. I am a river flower, a
Narcissus. I am glorious. I am the river winding through Seoul. I am fluid
and so is my fame, my splendor. Elegant, brave flowers always appear on
the surface of the water. Swim deep; dive through the mirror to harvest
the perpetual self. I am the eternal river, perpetuity of mirrors flowing
forever, outstanding, glorious echo, projection of reflections, swimming
deep in I, flooding, shining, liquid flower...

III: Wings

Maleficent

i.

in seventh grade I learned to pray
in Spanish is rezar

edged like razor,
work & worship,

I learned adoption
was life's sword:

maldición//malediction,
bendición//benediction,

doubled & edged beatitude
I should give thanks, I learned—

ii.

she left her blood
woven throughout. her curse,

benison, her hope, imprecation,
I learned

in high school, Latin cursus:
track, trajectory

swooping back. pendulum
defixio. to fix her, defix her;

to defix her, fix her. gladius,
sword of God, I raise

my voice, recite this oration//erasure,
as taught, to give

praise: gladiolus flower bowing
crimson in the pews. I learned

iii.

head bowed, do the work, the worship:
gladius dei. mater dei. kneel before

my saviors; savor gratitude. I learned
what words are twinned:

alma, soul; ala, wing. why cracking
open language never made for you

cleaves, gladius meus,
mater mea: pray, mother,

that you are not made-bad
making bad, not the bad-doer

doing bad works, that your
progeny can narrate, orate,

explain away the curse
with which you leveled

her: swoop of sword, swoop of wing.
ala, alma. ala, 엄마, I learned

iv.

magnificat anima mea Dominum,
exultavit spiritus meus in Deo

salutari meo, quia respexit humilitatem
ancillae suae; beatam me dicent omnes.

the swoop of these words,
her same-sided wings,

the rezar of my life,
it cut

Terra Nullius

"I did not know the walls of my birth mother's house,
or if she'd ever raised a child."
-Tracy O'Neill

I am a dislocated bone.

I am official documents in a manila folder.

I am inactive listserv emails.

I am in the process of, belonging.

If you claim me, you establish a precedent, of wanting.

Then you archive a dead community.

You pass judgment on me.

You stabilize me, snapping me into place.

For my 34th birthday

There are two kinds of dust. Two twins. I wear a lost twin around my wrist. Duality is a twin. There's old women and girls. No in-between. [   ], my land, the lamplight bursting around occupied hotel rooms in the flickering city, [   ]. It's a microaggression to ask where I'm from. Sea whispers, *You had too much poise for fifteen years on your first flight 'alone.' What broke when your mother shoved you from the nest?*

[   ], I am not exactly welcome in you. You incorporate me like a necessary evil, so much trash pressed to your white skin. [   ], you dropped me whole down your gullet, swallowing a gallon of Guinness and a chaser of soju to welcome (ambiguously) me. [   ] implies bearing myself, kayaking from mother's womb to another's welcome. Deslocamento, I'm translating this word as a type of movement, spatial uncentering, bewilderment. *Destabilization.* Don't lie and tell me I would have, you say now, would have been welcome to stay. A child born of two strangers' passion, ennui or desperation so thick it choked them, or so bodily, commonplace it existed to be quenched. Don't pretend you saved me and never assume you can bring me back. I simply moved chesslike, from one deslocamento, wretched

future, to another. I am my own twin. A Gemini of what-ifs suffering the night flight in darkness, lights on in the new city. Born twice, once this prideful month, once in October, taking my first breath in the [   ] International Terminal. Am I a boomerang who will come to rest in the hand of a mother, or a rock to be hurled at the sea in unwelcome?

I am a FedEx dispatch.
I am a telegram to a lover across the globe.
I am a chess   move and   countermove.
But when you ask me the simplest of ideas:
Where did you come from? Where were you born?
Where, where, where: I can say it in twelve languages
but I can never answer.

Adoption=/=Abortion

Reason for relinquishment: "…the natural mother realized her pregnancy too late and gave birth to the baby without any plan…"

fuck your mom
             "27/elementary school graduate/none/unwed"

your dad
             "32/junior high school graduate/peddler/unwed"

tell me without telling me my mom's a whore
                who "happened to get acquainted with"

these thin sheets of paper that show
                                        me as "adoptable"

why I wished to be
                                        an abortion

why my suicidal ideas weren't self-erasure but pain-erasure
                        throw out baby with bathwater

try to get through all the trauma even if the consequence is
                                                    you

back to nihilism
             an idea your mom should have contemplated

glorious void
             an idea your mom should have reconsidered

unthinking
                an idea not available to your mom

un-existing

                         an idea your mom didn't choose

for you, "healthy and cute"

                                 chosen anyway

baby girl

                            you parents' daughter

I do what I have to to live. I do what I have to, to live. I do what I have, too, to live. I do what I have to live. I have to live. I have to live I have to   she chose to have me live

Her & Me, 羽

she hid from me her   wings her every
thing   her shadows   covering up her
name she hid   from me   fairy tale
feathers   tale   dark in untelling tore
me   in egg   in utero   I am her
ugly duckling I   grew   apart I
searched for   others to be
long to   distance   lengthening   with time
longing   to re   claim

fledge I am become her
bard   singing nest   wings to un
do   first flight   recover   memories   re
deem   our tale   told   for myself
I   fashion swan 羽   han connection
strengthening   subjunctive fog
ala 엄마 ala
                  to
[what it will be//what I will be   ]

Frutti di mare

O ancestors   you who moved   to the sea
to the tides   who ate of   wave born
harvest   ate of   wars
wreckage   whatever was
caught   that day   you ingested   fresh
deluge   of blood   fracture   of border

I dedicate to you   this meal of oysters
packaged for consumption   like   my body   vessel
shipwrecked   lost   in currents & stars   dressed
in fermented juices   shucked   from one shell
to another   jurisdictional sea
Italian   American   Korean   American   cut open
my belly   read my entrails   ancestry
colatura di alici   gochujang   contested territory
terra nullius   O ancestors   let me return
to simpler times   let me eat of
your uncanned gifts   foreign
lunch   on   foreign coast

let me eat   what comes to me
what tide brings   what future sings

Adoptee Song

-For Lee Herrick and Adopted Feels workshop attendees

O almighty God pray for us adoptees
Now and at the hour of our rebirth

How even the most innocuous word choice can hurt
us—that's how we all became writers: truth
-tellers. Lie-tellers. Story-tellers.
How official documents drafted a life
that keeps revising, a viewpoint that keeps
distancing, eyes questing for emotion
in antique manila words, Cokes and Nikes to keep us
running. How can so many lies
join hands—you and I and you and I; how can the timbre
of *home Korea mother, father Korea home* smash my heart
like a cardboard box, broken rebuilt self restituted self

born of the virgin Mother and became human.
crucified under rule of law they suffered

Even the only place we're home in is each other.
We borrow each other's feelings—good neighbors sharing
the same lot. Braiding narrative kingdoms, storied
heroes with over-complex origins, we wear names
explosive, radioactive, adhesive
otherness trailing us capes. Escape to our gathering,
our chance to discard
viscose: this fine thread, this, this
acceptance isn't just for writers. We all wrote
into this story we ride; we from han winds
from han hands in han eyes

were buried. On the third day
they rose again in accordance with

55

Augustine took notes on the *Phaedo* and preached
all mortals have two horses, one Korean, one not.
That's us, yoked in two: an apology is sorry. It is
defense. It is two animals come together to move as one;
it is us in control. It is the lie that words move us,
blood moves us, Sulwhasoo moves us, sorrow moves us.
It is the lie that beauty is simple. What is rebuilt to survive
and does, exists. We must not fight to the death.
Look, the world is shining, slick and inimitable in the palm
of the Godhand. Look inside and say, I am not a tug of war.
I am not divided self. I am I am I live I live and let that echo
resonate through the divine you, the one you, the you I see
the I you see in me...

look forward to the resurrection of the dead
and the life of the world to come

susurration

you have a lot of poeting left in you.

you have a lot of poeming left in you.
left in you, poet, you left
poeming in your lot of having.

having left you, poeming, poet
-ing allotted you that lot,
that once you left. a lot left—

in your life lifting what you have,
poet, letting poems leave you.
a lot of poems enliven you,
let the life live in you.

lift up that which you do not have,
poet, poeming in you what has left.
having lived, once poems leave you,
your lot in life has lifted.

once, you left poems alive,
alight: the burn of sun,
the sting of salt,
the loving.

prayer to my guardian angel

in my childhood
bedroom
moon silvered,
birds caught fire at dawn,
light reflected in her face on the wall,
her eyes closed
willfully, Madonna,
mama.

she taught me to pray. what cannot be
narrated, orated, explained
away, I cried to her
at night, alone, while my parents
slept. told me always,
you must have faith.
in this thing, bigger than you, that God did
the right thing, that I did

[the right thing]

I ask
for answers

she will not answer,
she cannot answer. she
does not know
you

she prayed along with you
every night, that she did
the right thing, that God did
the right thing, that I do

Notes

The quote by Ursula K. LeGuin is from her novel *The Lathe of Heaven.*

The prayer to the guardian angel, "Angel of God," is a common Catholic prayer taught to children. The guardian angel is believed to be a divine watcher assigned to each human at birth.

This chapbook uses words from the following languages, in rough order of importance and recurrence: Korean (transliterated and in Hangul), Latin, Japanese, Spanish, Italian, Brazilian Portuguese, French and Mandarin Chinese. As intended, all can be either: understood from context, searched for definitions/translations, and/or engaged with sonically by the reader. As I am only a native speaker of English, all language mistakes are mine and mine alone—all translation semantics and intentionality are also mine and mine alone.

An American Tail is a 1986 movie by Don Bluth about a young immigrant who gets separated from his family and goes on a journey to find them again. The song "Somewhere Out There" by Linda Ronstadt and James Ingram, was the movie's most famous and well-known.

"1986 년 October" plays with Korean syntax in English and includes a retrograde abecedarian—that is, an abecedarian in which the English alphabet is out of order—as its middle stanza.

"The Ugly Duckling" is a popular fairy tale by Hans Christian Andersen, often republished in illustrated books for children.

Han is the word for what could be called the Korean spirit, a marker of Korean identity. No more excellent musing on this term has been put in English than Esther Ra's poem "(한)국 (han)kuk" from her chapbook, *book of untranslatable things.*

"History of Adoption in ~~Korea~~Maria" uses information from https://www.kadoption.or.kr/en/info/info_history.jsp, detailing the timeline, numbers of children, and revision of adoption practices and laws, while simultaneously papering over the erasure and denial of the existence of these Korean children by the government.

CEFR level refers to the Common Framework of Reference for Languages, a six-part scale meant to guide foreign language pedagogy and outcomes as set by the Council of Europe.

"Language Immersion" uses diction from the Eucharistic Prayer in Catholic Mass.

"Loki & me" contains riffs on lyrics from "Down with the Sickness" by Disturbed, as well as quotes from the MCU, mostly from *Thor* and *The Avengers*.

보다, the Korean word "to see" is inspired by the jisho.org dictionary entry for the same verb "to see" in Japanese (miru). The words and phrases in caps refer to the verb's semantic contextual usage.

영 is not only part of my Korean name, 수영, but also the word for "zero" among other meanings.

The word "hypnerotomachia" is from the famous medieval book *Hypnerotomachia Poliphili*, "The Strife of Love in a Dream," literally "sleep love fight" from the Greek. References in this poem to whalers come from the book *In the Heart of the Sea* by Nathaniel Philbrick.

"朝鮮姓名復舊令/조선 성명 복구/Name Restoration Order" utilizes diction from naming laws during and after the Japanese occupation. Korean people first were ordered to change their names and create surnames, which they often did by translating hanja (the Korean version of Chinese characters) to kanji (the Japanese version thereof) and trying to find a name in Japanese that matched the meaning or significance of their given and surnames. After the occupation, Koreans restored their names to Korean versions and began learning and speaking Korean once more, something that is addressed in books such as *DMZ Colony* by Don Mee-Choi and *Dictee* by Theresa Hak Kyung Cha. As an adoptee, the hanja version of my name and surname have been lost, so I have taken the contextual meanings of possible hanja characters to make the final section of this poem.

Lines from "Maleficent" come from the "Magnificat," "my soul magnifies the Lord" (Luke 1:46-55), a popular Catholic prayer and song.

The quotes from "Adoption=/=Abortion" are direct quotes from my adoption files. This poem was originally a contrapuntal to match "Antipodes." Please find it online and read it in that form.

Language in "Adoptee Song" originates in the Nicene Creed, a doctrinal statement accepted by many branches of Christianity and recited during Catholic Mass.

acknowledgements

Prior versions of these poems appeared in *Moonchild Magazine, Poets Reading the News, Tahoma Literary Magazine, Red Alder Review, Vox Viola, Pollux Journal, The Hellebore, jmww, Off Menu Press, Variant Lit, cream city review, Lucky Jefferson, Ice Floe Press, Brave Voices Magazine, Gordon Square Review, Typehouse,* and *Salamander.* I'm grateful to the editors and staff for believing in my work. Alana Saltz, Nadia Gerassimenko, and Aimee Suzara also lent their editorial eye to my poems.

This chapbook would not exist without the kindness, brilliance, and dedication of Josh Savory at Game Over Books and the GoB team. Many thanks to my blurbers, Lee Herrick and Diana Khoi Nguyen. Diane Ventre and Dimitri Reyes provided last-minute assistance and advice on a prior version of the manuscript, which GoB shepherded to its amazing final form.

Oormila Vijayakrishnan Prahlad, an amazing artist and writer, provided commissioned cover art for this project that went beyond my wildest dreams for the chap. Much love!

A big shoutout to my Lavender and Fig Group Poets—Abie, Lauren, Jessica, and Reina—D.E. Hardy, and other workshop groups, informal and formal, that I have been honored to be a part of. They have been seminal in shaping my poems.

Many thanks to the organizations and people that have supported me including Kenyon Review Writers Workshop, Tin House Workshop, Lighthouse Writers Workshop, GrubStreet Writers, Murphy Writers Workshop, The Speakeasy Project, Kundiman, Palm Beach Poetry Festival, Lit Cleveland, The Loft, HUES Foundation, Fine Arts Work Center, VONA/Voices, Hudson Valley Writers' Center, Proyecto 'ace, SAFTA, SCWA, The Juniper Institute, Adopted Feels, The Hambidge Center and The Watering Hole. A special thank you to Goddard College and my fiction communities, especially the '21-'22 Novel Generator and my Verge group, Karen R., Karen J., Monika, and Susanna, whose encouragement and critiques have kept me going.

To my lit mag communities especially at *ang(st)*, *Longleaf Review*, *Hanok Review*, *Uncharted Magazine*, *Foglifter*, *The Seventh Wave*, *Five Minutes*, and *Chestnut Review* and their editors, staff, and readers: thank you for you. You've made my life so much better through allowing me to serve.

To other adoptee, Korean, and Korean American writers, I stand beside you.

To my family and friends and my cat Minwu who are constantly supporting me in all that I need: thank you. This is a wound that is continually healed by your love.

To my birth mother, whose long and tender shadow is cast over my life, my work: I think of you. I love you. Tonight and every night.

biography

Maria S. Picone—수영—(she/her/hers) has four chapbooks, *Anti Asian Bias* (forthcoming Game Over Books), *Adoptee Song* (Game Over Books), *This Tenuous Atmosphere* (Conium), and *Korean Girl Ghost* (self-published). Maria is the recipient of an Emerging Artist Grant from the South Carolina Arts Commission. She won Cream City Review's Summer 2020 Poetry Prize and Salamander's Louisa Solano Memorial Emerging Poet Award, for which she published her debut e-chapbook *Water Gwisin Saves the Earth*. Her work has been supported by Lighthouse Writers, GrubStreet, VONA, Kenyon Review, The Watering Hole, Tin House, South Arts, South Carolina Arts Commission, and Juniper Summer Writers. She attended Hambidge as a Leaders in the Arts Distinguished Fellow. She is the managing editor of *Chestnut Review* and edits at *Uncharted Mag*, *Foglifter*, *Five Minutes*, and *The Seventh Wave*. She holds an MFA in fiction from Goddard College and degrees from Princeton, Rice, and Western New Mexico University. You can read her work in *Salamander*, *Reckoning*, *Orca Lit*, *The Good Life Review*, and *Best Small Fictions* among others.

www.ingramcontent.com/pod-product-compliance
Lightning Source LLC
Chambersburg PA
CBHW060353130626
46553CB00003B/1210